**ALARA Inc. Monograph Series
No. 3**

Donors as stakeholders in Community-Based Participatory Action Research: Praxis as typology in framing their roles

Zermarie Deacon, Ph.D.
University of Oklahoma

David Moxley, Ph.D.
University of Oklahoma

Monograph Series edited by Eileen Piggot-Irvine
Royal Roads University, Victoria BC, Canada

Published by

Action Learning, Action Research Association

2012

2nd Reprint 2020

Biographical Statement:
Zermarie Deacon is an assistant professor of Human Relations and Women's and Gender Studies at the University of Oklahoma, Norman. David Moxley is the Oklahoma Health Care Authority Professor and a Professor of Social Work. He is affiliated with the Anne and Henry Zarrow School of Social Work at the University of Oklahoma, Norman. All correspondence should be addressed to the first author at Zermarie@ou.edu or, via mail, at Department of Human Relation, 601 Elm Avenue, PHSC 729, Norman, OK 73019

Key Words: Community Based Participatory Action Research, funding CBPAR, donors, CBPAR methods so bring them into the process of fund development. This may result in a modification to the ways in which future participants and donors interact in order to leverage the potential power of CBPAR.

Through the organization of our experience with donors in CBPAR, we identified four types of donors: Type 1 donor (engaged with a strong perspective); Type 11 donor (engaged with a weak perspective); Type 111 donor (disengaged with a strong perspective); and Type 1V donor (disengaged with a weak perspective). Each type of donor has a different relationship to participants of CBPAR and has a different impact upon the kind of research and inquiry that participants conduct. We provide brief examples of each type of donor.

A Cautionary Tale: Considerations for Resource Development in CBPAR Contexts

Our experiences with various types of donors illustrate the importance of taking the donor's perspective into consideration when planning and executing CBPAR. The reality is that eventually most research and action requires more funding than is likely available locally. However, the process of applying for and/or accepting funding may require significant trade-offs participants or stakeholders must make in terms of the CBPAR process. These trade-offs may start as early as the process of identifying donors who are willing to support the work to be completed. In other cases, research and action may be designed specifically in response to donor priorities and may or may not reflect true community needs. We argue that by considering donor types, CBPAR participants may be best positioned to leverage donor funding in such a way as to support their overarching aims.

Conclusion: Implications for Theory and Practice in CBPAR

CBPAR participants may treat those organizations that provide funding in support of their research and action as silent partners in the research process. However, the truth is that donors can exact a significant influence on the CBPAR process, and their involvement should be problematized. The decision to seek outside funding is thus not one that should be taken lightly. Rather, decisions regarding the kinds of donors with whom they are willing to engage in order to retain the integrity of the participatory process are central to the viability of CBPAR projects. Additionally, rather than relinquishing significant power over the CBPAR process to donors, participants should assist donors to honor the democratic principles inherent in participatory research and action.

An awareness of the impact that donors have on CBPAR may have significant implications for the ways in which community members and their research partners go about applying for funding in order to support their work. Including donors as participants ensures that applicants for funding are significantly more strategic about their decisions to pursue funding, the kinds of funding sources they consider, and the ways in which they utilize funding. This understanding may additionally have implications for the ways in which donors interact with participants and the kinds of funding they offer. As such, including donors as participants impacts both CBPAR strategy as well as long-term sustainability of projects.

Executive Summary

Introduction

While the Community-Based Participatory Action Research (CBPAR) literature is extensive, it does not adequately explore the donor-participant relationship. In this monograph, we argue that the future of CBPAR can be strengthened if donor roles as participants in this form of research and action can be better elucidated, community participants and academic partners can be more deliberate in their decisions to pursue external funding and include donors as partners in their work, and thereby make the potential of the donor-participant relationship and its consequences explicit for all stakeholders. We argue that these considerations ensure better leveraging of the potential power of CBPAR.

CBPAR shows significant promise as a form of research and action that may be successfully leveraged in order to address significant social issues. However, this form of inquiry requires adherence to particular sets of values and often deviates from the format followed by more conventional research paradigms. CBPAR has significant resource requirements that often fall outside of the capacity of communities. Thus while CBPAR may have significant promise as a form of research that could help donors advance their social change aims, participants in this form of inquiry and action often have a complicated relationship with the donor community. In this monograph we argue that this relationship has not been sufficiently explored. We argue that donors have a significant impact upon the kind of CBPAR partners may undertake as well as the ways in which this kind of research and action is executed. Hence, we argue that the impact donors have upon CBPAR should be further examined. We propose a typology of donors and examine the impact of each donor type upon CBPAR.

Method

For this investigation, we reflexively draw upon our own experiences as practitioners of CBPAR, offering praxis in the form of a typology of donors. We engaged in a process of reflection and critical thinking. This was followed by mutual engagement and documentation of our own experiences and the insights into the donor-recipient dynamic we gained from a consideration of the multiple CBPAR projects in which we played key roles. What emerged from this process was a donor typology intended to inform CBPAR projects, practitioners, and participants about how donors may influence their aims, methods, knowledge development objectives, and utilization efforts.

Donor typology as praxis

Through reflexivity, we consider "learning in action" to be a salient ingredient of our achievement of insight into the role of donors in CBPAR projects. We are not using the typology to assert a general perspective - we construct it as an example of how to bridge our first person experience in CBPAR with a theoretical perspective on the role of donors in CBPAR projects, although others may find the typology useful in their own work, and may seek to modify it based on their own first person experience.

The typology acts as a roadmap, a strategic tool - as in consciously shaping how future participants may come to think about and engage donors as potential CBPAR participants. The formulation of a tool like this demonstrates how strategy can emerge first from reflexivity and second from praxis: participants, particularly those whose statuses are marginalized, and too often are not seen by people in power as legitimate researchers themselves, can make the donor role explicit and then evaluate whether and to what degree they should engage such powerful sources of influence in their projects. Through such an explicit dialogue (which can also serve as a form of reflexivity), participants can frame expectations they possess for donor participants and so bring them into the process of fund development. This may result in a modification to the ways in which future participants and donors interact in order to leverage the potential power of CBPAR.

Through the organization of our experience with donors in CBPAR, we identified four types of donors: Type 1 donor (engaged with a strong perspective); Type 11 donor (engaged with a weak perspective); Type 111 donor (disengaged with a strong perspective); and Type 1V donor (disengaged with a weak perspective). Each type of donor has a different relationship to participants of CBPAR and has a different impact upon the kind of research and inquiry that participants conduct. We provide brief examples of each type of donor.

A Cautionary Tale: Considerations for Resource Development in CBPAR Contexts

Our experiences with various types of donors illustrate the importance of taking the donor's perspective into consideration when planning and executing CBPAR. The reality is that eventually most research and action requires more funding than is likely available locally. However, the process of applying for and/or accepting funding may require significant trade-offs participants or stakeholders must make in terms of the CBPAR process. These trade-offs may start as early as the process of identifying donors who are willing to support the work to be completed. In other cases, research and action may be designed specifically in response to donor priorities and may or may not reflect true community needs. We argue that by considering donor types, CBPAR participants may be best positioned to leverage donor funding in such a way as to support their overarching aims.

Conclusion: Implications for Theory and Practice in CBPAR

CBPAR participants may treat those organizations that provide funding in support of their research and action as silent partners in the research process. However, the truth is that donors can exact a significant influence on the CBPAR process, and their involvement should be problematized. The decision to seek outside funding is thus not one that should be taken lightly. Rather, decisions regarding the kinds of donors with whom they are willing to engage in order to retain the integrity of the participatory process are central to the viability of CBPAR projects. Additionally, rather than relinquishing significant power over the CBPAR process to donors, participants should assist donors to honor the democratic principles inherent in participatory research and action.

An awareness of the impact that donors have on CBPAR may have significant implications for the ways in which community members and their research partners go about applying for funding in order to support their work. Including donors as participants ensures that applicants for funding are significantly more strategic about their decisions to pursue funding, the kinds of funding sources they consider, and the ways in which they utilize funding. This understanding may additionally have implications for the ways in which donors interact with participants and the kinds of funding they offer. As such, including donors as participants impacts both CBPAR strategy as well as long-term sustainability of projects.

Table of Contents

List of Tables

Abstract

Recognizing the novelty of community based participatory action research (CBPAR), potential donors may be skeptical of the models, processes, and forms of research this genre incorporates in working with communities and those constituencies that are too often omitted from the governance of research. Participatory forms of action research pose their own resource requirements, which may differ from more traditional forms of social research, particularly in the early stages of inquiry. This monograph explores the impact of the donor perspective, donor types, and corresponding levels of engagement on CBPAR research. Accordingly, the impact that donors have upon the kind of participatory inquiry that is planned and executed is likely taken for granted and never evaluated. This is especially problematic given the value-based nature of CBPAR and its emphasis upon democratic processes in research planning and administration. The application for, and receipt of, external funding may either support or undermine this accepted system of values. Practitioners of CBPAR should be aware of this impact. Conversely, donors may be unaware of the ways in which they can uniquely leverage CBPAR in order to achieve their own social change goals. The principal focus of the proposed monograph is thus to facilitate an awareness of the impact that donors have on CBPAR as well as to outline ways in which donors and participants can better collaborate in order to leverage the potential of this form of inquiry. Following an overview of the CBPAR model and relevant action research methodology we use to advance our understanding of the donor typology, we (a) offer an overview of the four types of donors, (b) consider the influence of each of the four donors on the direction and feasibility of CBPAR, (c) outline implications for working with donors across the continuum of types, and (d) make suggestions for improving the donor-participant collaboration.

Introduction

While the Community-Based Participatory Action Research (CBPAR) literature is extensive, it does not adequately explore the donor-participant relationship. In this monograph, we argue that CBPAR can be strengthened if practitioners can better understand donor roles as participants in this form of research. In this way, community participants and academic partners can be more deliberate in their decisions to pursue external funding and to include donors as partners in their work thereby making the potential of the donor-participant relationship and its consequences explicit for all stakeholders. We argue that these considerations ensure better leveraging of the potential power of CBPAR while protecting the distinctiveness of this form of research and action. This additionally allows donors to best target their resources on achieving objectives they value.

By donors we refer to those entities, whether public or private, that finance research and intervention activities to achieve their own philanthropic, service, knowledge development, or strategic aims. We argue that the donor perspective is important to consider because of their significant influence, particularly as they mobilize and extend their conceptions of what is appropriate, deploy values, and otherwise shape and form externally funded social action. Thus, given the centrality of reflexivity and praxis within CBPAR, those who value this kind of inquiry should remain mindful of how donor intent and aims can influence projects, and how projects can influence donors. This has important implications for the future of CBPAR praxis.

Donors are a pivotal stakeholder group whose role participants and researchers may ignore or downplay the process of securing necessary resources, but who nonetheless play a significant, if not controlling, part in shaping and developing CBPAR in its inception and throughout the process of inquiry. Donors additionally often have social change or other goals in mind that may be well served by partnering more effectively with CBPAR participants. However, this potential may not be well understood by either donors or CBPAR participants and may thus remain untapped or go unaddressed during crucial phases of inquiry and action within real life community settings.

The purpose of this monograph is to enlighten both recipients of funding and donors about how they can better position themselves in order to render CBPAR more productive, protect if not advance the distinctive qualities of CBPAR, and collaborate to advance responsive and engaged research in local communities. We conceive of the donor-recipient interaction as a partnership in which both parties can evaluate whether funding is most appropriate given the intent and potential impact of CBPAR projects. Thus, while we focus on each party within the funding transaction we remain mindful that the relationship is a reciprocal one in which both recipients and donors can grow and develop in meaningful ways through their interaction.

We intend this monograph for donors, recipients, and participants in CBPAR, as well as researchers who all share a concern for producing useful knowledge for the public good. As such, we consider (from the experience we garnered within the crucible of CBPAR projects) the potential influence of donors on the formulation, initiation, and implementation of CBPAR. In different sections we address CBPAR participants and partners who are searching for resources to achieve their ends, as well as donors whose purpose may be best actualized by funding CBPAR projects. We end with recommendations for ways in which future CBPAR praxis can be modified in order to ensure a harmonious and ultimately productive relationship between donors and CBPAR values.

Community-Based Participatory Action Research (CBPAR) in Context

Participatory Action Research

Kurt Lewin (1946, 1948) and later Argyris and his colleagues (1985) framed action research. Lewin (1946; 1948) amplified the influence of context on knowledge development by emphasizing the relationship of subject and object and of observer and event that occur within a context of inquiry in which knowledge would be applied for the purposes of social betterment. While the Lewinian (1946; 1948) form of action research underscored the important linkage of investigator and action, the evolution of action research into participatory forms further elaborates the importance of multiple perspectives in inquiry. Participatory action research recognizes that there is a plurality of perspectives that not only influence how a particular phenomenon is experienced but how such experience can shape inquiry and generate innovation in method, theory, and utilization.

Participatory action research emerges alongside emancipatory views of social science that critically examine the traditional dominance of a sole investigator; one who likely incorporates the dominant doctrine of a given field (Israel, Schulz, Parker & Becker, 1998; Smith, 2005). This form of research and action recognizes the importance of giving primacy to the perspective of those who are not dominant and who typically are omitted from inquiry at all stages (i.e. the conception, design, implementation, and utilization phases; Gaventa, 1993). Israel and her colleagues additionally amplify the importance of participation, control, and influence by those who have been traditionally omitted from the process of inquiry; typically those who are not seen as qualified researchers (Israel et al., 1998). Thus, while Lewin's (1946; 1948) original conception of action research linked perspective, action, and knowledge, participatory action research amplifies the importance of minority perspective as a vital influence in shaping both inquiry and utilization of findings as forms of action intended to generate social change.

Community based participatory action research is a form of research that aims to generate social change within particular communities. It involves community members as equal participants with researchers and aims to generate positive social change and to improve community health, broadly defined. This form of action research has increasingly come to represent the hallmark of effective and ethical research intended to effect positive change in communities (e.g., Foster-Fishman, Nowell, Deacon, Nievar, & McCann, 2005; Harper, Bangi, Contreras, Pedraza, Toliver, & Vess, 2004; Savan, 2004).

Typically the focus of CBPAR is on local conditions and how those influence the wellbeing of underrepresented or disempowered groups. By melding participation, action, and inquiry, those local conditions can potentially change for the better, which may in turn creates positive feedback strengthening motivation, increasing assertiveness, and elevating the power of participants. Thus, change for the better in local conditions may result from such synergy (Foster-Fishman, et al, 2005; Harper, 2004; Israel, et al, 1998; Savan, 2004).

The Nature of CBPAR

Multiple models guide community-based participatory inquiry, testifying to the diversity of this paradigm. However, notably, the unifying threads that run through all of these models is the importance of prioritizing the perspective of a given community in problem definition and intervention design and respecting the primacy of community benefit to be derived from all research activities (e.g., Foster-Fishman, et al, 2005; Garvin, 1995; Israel et al., 1998; Quigley, 2006). Indeed, for the CBPAR researcher, obtaining useful and action-oriented knowledge through the extensive involvement of participants may assume priority over the more traditional aspects of rigor.

The fact that this form of inquiry includes community members as equal research partners with the researchers themselves demonstrates the emphasis CBPAR places upon the participation and involvement of those individuals who historically have been excluded from a central role in the knowledge-generation process. Proximity to, immersion in, and primary experience with serious social issues mean that those individuals, groups and whole communities who possess this kind of knowledge can add immeasurably to the research process and to subsequent knowledge development. As such, community-based participatory inquiry is conducted for the benefit of the community and encourages social justice (Israel, et al, 1998) with useful knowledge emerging within such a context. Community-based participatory research is additionally aimed at directly or indirectly empowering community members and assisting them in the development of new skills, roles, and capacities (e.g., Foster-Fishman, Fitzgerald, Brandell, Nowell, Chavis, & Van Egeren, 2006; Foster-Fishman, et al, 2005; Garvin, 1995; Savan, 2004). This form of research is thus unabashedly value-based, and is a form of inquiry that acknowledges the importance of those values that strengthen the status of people who too often are outsiders in most research projects as well as in the larger society.

Some have argued that all forms of participatory inquiry require investigators to make explicit their values relative to the work in which they engage. Encouraging such reflexivity on the part of investigators directly recognizes the value-based nature of this form of inquiry (Miller & Shinn, 2005). This additionally strengthens 'action' as a critical aspect of participatory inquiry by potentially contributing to the generation of value-informed, positive social change within those communities that serve as hosts of the research (Foster-Fishman, et al, 2005; Garvin, 1995; Israel, 1998; Miller & Shinn, 2005; Savan, 2004). CBPAR investigators thus do not stand alone in the research process and refrain from objectifying the contexts in which they work and distance themselves from those who struggle with problematic local conditions (Feen-Calligan, Washington, & Moxley, 2009; Foster-Fishman, et al, 2005; Garvin, 1995; Harper, 2004; Israel, et al, 1998; Quigley, 2006; Savan, 2004; Washington & Moxley, 2008). CBPAR researchers are not pure investigators in the traditional sense. They are colleagues and fellow participants aligned with research participants or, more accurately, research producers and utilizers, whose social status is typically low (Foster-Fishman, et al, 2005; Israel, et al, 1998; Miller & Shinn, 2005).

CBPAR's unique potential to contribute to positive social change within marginalized communities serves as a powerful tool in harnessing social change, particularly in local contexts, ones which may experience considerable institutional neglect at higher systems and political levels. The strength of this method lies in its potential to foster community members' understanding of the local conditions they face as well as of those strengths that may be drawn upon in order to ensure the success of interventions. CBPAR is additionally consistent with asset approaches emerging within community development, the helping professions, and among those offering self-help and mutual support. The asset perspective recognizes how a diversity of strengths and assets operate in local communities and their mobilization can facilitate the leveraging of action to further improve quality of life within a given community (Green & Haines, 2012).

We communicate the distinctiveness of the CBPAR model through the content of Table 1 (Boeck, Moxley, Wachter, & Rosenthal, 2010). The model identifies the key elements of CBPAR projects as possessing the values of mutual respect, trust, relationship formation, and commitment to action, that is, social betterment. Simply put, it takes time to enact such values and allow them to shape a given project. The table also highlights potential stages forming the participatory dimension. The dimension incorporates an initial form of engagement that can formalize a project in preparation for action focusing on social betterment. Sustainability is a final product of this process as the project gains enough structure, content, and resources to continue operation after passing through previous stages in which ongoing sustainability is uncertain.

Table 1: CBPAR model.

	Stage of Participation			
	Engagement	Formalization	Action	Sustainability
Core Elements				
Mutual Respect	Understanding aging and positive aging and the kind of knowledge participants seek through NANAP	Formalizing roles within a coordinating structure within the project	Consulting with one another before taking action; consensual action	Socializing newcomers into the practices of the participation and collaboration
Trust	Consistent involvement in partnership and community	Adhering to agreed upon norms of interaction and agreed upon road map	Adhering to the action plan until there is change based on consensual decisions regarding design priorities	Expanding mutually beneficial outcomes
Relationship Formation	Getting to know one and accept one another as individuals	Consistent positive interaction among members within the project structure	Community members and university personnel working together collaboratively	Succession planning and socialization of leaders and members into critical roles
Commitment to Action	Agreeing on purpose, aims, and vision	Formulating a joint work plan	Mutual assessment and evaluation of action	Continuous strategic planning for sustaining collaboration

Rationale for Considering Donors in CBPAR

Increasingly CBPAR is employed to inform externally funded intervention development as well as to achieve the aims of basic and applied research (Flicker, Savan, McGrath, Kolenda, & Mildenberger, 2008; Savan, 2004; Savan, Flicker, Kolenda, & Mildenberger, 2009). However, despite this trend, the influence or impact donors have upon participatory inquiry is simply underappreciated. This is significant given the potential magnitude of their roles, the potency of their perspectives, and the centrality of their resources. Many researchers, even those who endorse participation as an ethical and epistemological necessity, may simply assign considerable power to donors, or may ignore how donors shape research early on, particularly in its conception, and later when a design undergoes implementation.

This oversight is an important one given the potentially significant influence of donor values upon inquiry. Donors come in many different forms, operate under various auspices (e.g., corporate or government), and represent different motivational factors in their research aims;

some prioritizing knowledge development in the traditional research paradigm, while others seek to blend knowledge production and social betterment. Others pursue funding aims to strengthen their strategic positions within communities or markets, such as corporations. To achieve their aims, donors create specific programmatic initiatives offering resources to potential researchers. In turn, those undertaking inquiry may adjust to the value set, perspectives, and priorities of a given funding source. By making explicit this relationship and its potential implications, we aim to encourage greater reflexivity with regard to the future directions of community-based participatory action research. In this way donor funding can be optimally leveraged to more effectively generate social change.

Conventional research paradigms likely inform much of donor-funded CBPAR. Those paradigms do not necessarily value true collaboration between donors and participants, nor recognize just how important collaboration is among participants who often are of diverse backgrounds or whose backgrounds include experiences of minority or devalued status. Rather, donors likely want to inform if not specify significant aspects of funded CBPAR. Donors may not fund key aspects or stages of CBPAR such as relationship development or capacity building phases, which may take considerable time, require considerable investment of process-related effort, and require nurturance before more specific aspects of research come into play. A better understanding of the theoretical as well as practical implications of CBPAR as well as the ways in which this form of inquiry and action can advance donors' goals may improve collaborations between community participants and donors.

Protection of Precarious Values

Given its complexity and uniqueness, CBPAR is based upon a value-system that many donors and researchers may frankly find alien. The uninitiated, or those groups that do not recognize the core values of this paradigm, may simply discount values that inform engagement, relationship formation, trust building, and mutual support. This may represent an obstacle for effective CBPAR research. Pairing an indigenous understanding of a particular setting with the resources donors provide and the knowledge regarding research and intervention development brought to the table by researchers may illuminate in meaningful ways important aspects of social problems. However, this form of inquiry and action may be fragile and otherwise unstable, particularly in the early period of its formation, so it is essential for all stakeholders, and powerful stakeholders in particular, to work towards the protection of the precarious values inherent in CBPAR. If powerful stakeholders do not understand or appreciate these values, this may threaten the integrity of a given CBPAR project.

By virtue of their potentially significant power, donors, in particular, may easily subvert the CBPAR process, perhaps not even knowing what is at stake. Those donors that do not value or understand the participatory aspects of CBPAR may demand to control so much of the process that the true value of the participatory model is lost. This is especially true in situations where donors do not understand the potential value of CBPAR for the achievement of their goals or where they adhere so strongly to their own set of values regarding research and intervention development that they are unwilling to make the accommodations necessary for the success of CBPAR. The power that donors possess, which is uninformed by the core values of CBPAR, can undermine the spirit and substance of the participatory process inherent in this form of action research. It is, therefore, essential for donors to understand the ways in which they can leverage CBPAR for their own benefit and, paradoxically, to be educated regarding the ways in which they can assist in protecting other CBPAR participants against their own overuse of power. In this sense, donors become one more potentially influential stakeholder group in a complex multi-group field in which members are negotiating the essential aspects of a given community research effort.

The Resource Requirements of CBPAR

The resource needs that go along with a successful CBPAR project is yet another area in which donors who are unfamiliar with the CBPAR process may require education. As discussed above, CBPAR projects have different requirements than do basic and even some applied or developmental research projects. CBPAR requires significant early work in order to establish relationships among community members and researchers to lay the foundation for the ensuing collaboration.

This phase of the work may take the form of multiple meetings and opportunities for stakeholders to get to know one another better and to jointly outline requisite work that possesses significance for all participants. Such early work can culminate in the emergence of a governance structure for a project imbuing it with policies and procedures for its future work. This phase allows all stakeholders to approach the research and development process as equal partners who, while each may possess a different perspective, may find unity in the goal of social betterment.

The initial phases of CBPAR also often involve a capacity building component so that community members are able to participate in the research and development process as equal partners to the socially more powerful members. While community members are experts on their communities, and should be respected as such, they often do not have the requisite knowledge and experience to engage in research and development although they can acquire such knowledge with the support and assistance of technical assistance, training, and collaborative projects. Many donors are unwilling or hesitant to provide funding for these unique aspects of CBPAR, representing a significant obstacle to the progress of community-based projects.

The Impact of Donors' Perspectives

Notably, and in spite of the open acknowledgement of the value-based nature of this form of research and intervention development, and the possibly important role that donors play, the impact of donors' perspective on CBPAR has had little consideration. While to date a handful of publications discuss the impact of funding priorities on research, these are primarily focused in the physical sciences, and are mostly intended to assist applicants in procuring funding (e.g., Buccola, Ervin, & Yang, 2009). The focus on obtaining funding for CBPAR research tends to be upon finding ways to encourage participants to become better able to conform to donor expectations and to accommodate funding cycles and processes (e.g., Flicker, et al, 2008; Plumb, Price, & Kavanaugh-Lynch, 2004; Savan, et al, 2009).

We argue that this lack of focus on donor priorities is tantamount to ignoring the proverbial 'elephant in the room'. If those involved in CBPAR search for external resources or funds to support community-based inquiry, then donors are salient stakeholders in any CBPAR project. So the values those individuals, groups, and institutions insert into the process (or assert) can very likely shape the agenda of inquiry in substantial and important ways.

As a result, donor priorities clearly have multiple and significant implications for research and intervention development. Those priorities likely play a significant role in shaping the kinds of research and intervention development efforts in which universities may engage, the kinds of communities and community organizations with which university researchers choose to partner, and the ways in which CBPAR is executed. This may be true whether or not a given project is already underway and requires funding to continue or whether a new project is being conceptualized, possibly in response to a call for proposals. Donor priorities may consequently influence both existing CBPAR projects as well as the kinds of new initiatives that are undertaken or not undertaken. To unpack the potential impact that donors have upon CBPAR is thus essential.

Recognizing this pivotal role that donors can play, we offer a typology of donors that incorporates two dimensions, (a) the strength of a donor's perspective on CBPAR, and (b) the donor's degree of engagement in the process of design and implementation. We elaborate how those two dimensions can form four alternative theoretical types. The four alternatives place into context the potential donor roles that investigators may want to consider as they design projects, assemble applications for external support, and implement their research. This framework also informs the ways in which donors and community and academic partners can more effectively collaborate in order to generate the desired outcomes of participatory research, which often has an aim of social betterment. We envision this typology as adding to our understanding of CBPAR praxis and as developing practitioners', researchers', and donors' understanding of the ways in which this form of research and action evolves.

Reflexive Methods of Theory Formation

Over the course of three months we (the authors) engaged in an iterative process including both discussion and written reflection. Early on we pursued several objectives to achieve a collaborative relationship using reflexive methods of mutual engagement. Here, by reflexivity, we mean a growing mutual appreciation of those experiences offering a common base of knowledge in addressing donor related themes in our own work, and comparing and contrasting those themes in our quest to surface an emergent theoretical framework of donor types.

Eight assertions steered our conception of the donor-CBPAR nexus - ones which helped us consider the potential typology using our own fairly consistent ways of thinking about theory development in CBPAR - that each case of CBPAR illuminated something distinct about the role of donors in the initiation, design, implementation, and subsequent development of a CBPAR project. The following are coordinating assertions guiding our further development of the typology in a reflexive and collaborative manner. Rather than distilling them from the literature, we drew them from our own CBPAR experience.

1. CBPAR projects often seek donor involvement and resource investments when they determine that they cannot fulfill their own aspirations for action and knowledge using their existing resources.

2. CBPAR projects can form in response to donor priorities and the related availability of funding for particular types of initiatives, although they are more likely emergent, take form in the crucible of the challenges communities face, and then participants search for resources outside of the community if they are unavailable internally.

3. Each potential donor possesses a distinctive stance toward knowledge and they adhere to a particular form of inquiry as the best means for producing the knowledge it values. The resources they offer community-based projects help them, the donors, actualize the knowledge they value.

4. Donors vary in how they translate their distinctive stance on knowledge into particular expectations of their own engagement, and assert this distinctive stance as a perspective - perhaps a controlling one on a given project.

5. It is up to the CBPAR collaborative to seek out donors, discover how to fulfill donor expectations, and engage in requisite resource development competencies so they can achieve those outcomes they value.

6. CBPAR collaboratives may be formed in response to donor priorities and can adjust their goals accordingly, perhaps reducing their distinctiveness or even compromising their integrity. The CBPAR collaborative can thus reflexively prioritize donor values over their own.

7. Actions CBPAR collaboratives take to achieve success in securing resources from external donors can consciously or unconsciously compromise their values or the higher order values

of CBPAR. Thus, the resource development process illuminates the precarious nature of CBPAR values in donor-project transactions.

We consider our process of knowledge formation indicative of investigator praxis, integrating our own practice experience with our propensities as academics to engage in concept and theory formation and subsequent action to construct a framework of donor types. We were mindful that while our own cases influence this process of theorizing, we were taking some liberty with concept formation. However, we purposefully sought to construct a theory of sorts through the empirical mapping (achieved through dialogue) of our own case rich experience and of the commonalities that unified our experiences with donors within CBPAR contexts. For such a process dialogic interaction is critical, particularly for enlightenment purposes, since we were seeking to make tacit knowledge explicit by structuring it as a schematic representation. The multiple discussions we held seeking to understand this dynamic were not trivial since such dialogue is very much central to the process of discovery in any venue of science (Bohm, 1994).

Still, as we considered what we knew about donors and how we came to know about them from our own experience, we engaged in what can be considered an action learning cycle, as Senge and his colleagues frame it (Senge et al., 2008). Through the exchange process we came to sense the possibility that engagement of donors and the perspective of donors were important dimensions in defining the donors' potential roles in CBPAR projects. We then structured those two dimensions by matching them with experience in almost a case study format. Such presencing, as Senge and his colleagues (2008) define it, facilitates the emergence of action found in a third step of realization. To bring the framework into conceptual form was the essence of realization.

We found the 2X2 matrix (see Table 2) to be particularly useful since it enabled us to portray the donor types in an elegant and meaningful way. Praxis here meant the melding or blending of professional engagement in CBPAR, personal experience with a range of cases, mutual and interactive reflection on our work, and the framing and organization of concepts to form a heuristic, that is, a theory to support reflection, planning, and subsequent practice. The formation of the framework was very much a product of a linkage of practice and theory. Then we validated the framework using other examples to test the classification scheme we offer in Table 2. While we recognize how cells can blur, we were able to generate enough examples within each cell to justify their differentiation into four types based on the intersection of two factors: donor engagement and strength of donor perspective.

The Donor Typology as Praxis

Integration of Practice and Theory

Through reflexivity, we consider 'learning in action' to be a salient ingredient of our achievement of insight into the role of donors in CBPAR projects. We are not using the typology to assert a general perspective - we construct it as an example of how to bridge our first person experience in CBPAR with a theoretical perspective on the role of donors in CBPAR projects, although others may find the typology useful in their own work, and may seek to modify it based on their own first person experience.

The typology itself illuminates how experienced CBPAR investigators engage in praxis as a product of multiple projects and of reflexivity in their engagement of one another as experienced participants in CBPAR. Practice and theory combine in this form of knowledge as a way to generate the two dimensions - engagement and perspective. We came to appreciate that donors differ in the strength of their perspective as to what they expect of CBPAR. Here donors may be quite controlling (and therefore possess a strong perspective) on how best to undertake the research they fund, or they may relinquish control to participants themselves in specifying the aims and process of the research.

Engagement for us came to mean the degree of involvement the donor takes within a given project. Some donors may seek to achieve a high level of engagement in a given CBPAR project so they can either experience the process as a source of their own learning or control the process itself, ensuring that their aims are met. Or, they may function in a rather disengaged manner reflecting the distance they wish to establish in relationship to a project they fund.

Early in our discussion we decided to make the two concepts orthogonal - as independent of one another. We saw both as important, as operative within the cases we reviewed and about which we dialogued, and each concept contributed a distinctive way of understanding the role of donors in CBPAR projects. Together the four cells serve as a roadmap offering users guidance in how to think through the implications of donor role, and useful in working closely with other participants in CBPAR projects in framing the potential or actual roles of donors.

Finally, we included a discussion of consonance and dissonance between donors and participants in order to illustrate the ways in which donor perspectives may intersect or diverge from those of participants. This further illustrates the ways in which perspective intersects with degree of engagement. An analysis of consonance and dissonance allows for a more in-depth illustration of the impact of donor perspectives on CBPAR as it allows for an illustration of the interplay between the two dimensions and donor relationships to CBPAR.

Thus, the framework is a strategic tool - as in consciously shaping how future participants may come to think about and engage donors as potential CBPAR participants. The formulation of a tool like this demonstrates how strategy can emerge first from reflexivity and second from praxis. Participants, particularly those whose statuses are marginalized and too often are not seen by people in power as legitimate researchers themselves, can make the donor role explicit and then evaluate whether and to what degree they should engage in their projects such powerful sources of influence. Through such a conscious dialogue (which can also serve as a form of reflexivity), participants can frame an explicit set of expectations they possess for donor participants and so bring them into the process of fund development. This may result in a modification of the ways in which future participants and donors interact to leverage the potential power of CBPAR.

In our discussions we identified other potential dimensions a future version of this typology could incorporate, including the size of the donor, societal location, such as corporation, foundation, university, or government, and scope, involving whether the donor is local, subnational, national, or international. As readers will see, we incorporate several of these factors into the brief examples we offer in a subsequent section, however, we leave it up to future researchers and practitioners to develop this typology further in order to highlight other ways in which the participant-donor relationship can be understood and optimally leveraged.

Four Types of Donors

We use the terms 'donor orientation' and 'participant orientation' in order to illustrate the ways in which donors and participants approach one another based upon the donor type and the implications this has for CBPAR.

Type I Donor (Engaged with Strong Perspective)

Donor orientation. The donor is well motivated to engage in the project and recognizes its relevance or value to learning from a given CBPAR project. The donor likely has a particular form of social action or learning objective in mind which they believe can be realized through funding a particular project. The donor may or may not also have a strong methodological orientation.

Participant orientation. Similarly, participants easily form and maintain a collegial relationship with the donor in designing and implementing all phases of the project. The CBPAR strategy is to keep the donor interested, supportive, and motivated to learn from the project. The project personnel may view the donor as an essential stakeholder who has a right to influence the project, but not to control it. Helping the donor learn from the project is an essential objective here.

Consonance. This donor can benefit significantly from CBPAR and if they understand the potential of this method of inquiry and action, can be powerful allies and participants. In this case, if the donor and community participants have a shared goal they can mobilize resources to effectively generate the change that both parties have in mind. This donor will likely fund the initial phases of CBPAR that differ from more traditional research paradigms and may contribute to the development of a powerful CBPAR project.

Dissonance. In the event that the donor is highly invested, yet does not understand or otherwise appreciate the power and value of CBPAR, this type of donor can be a significant detriment to a CBPAR project. While this donor has a strong perspective on the kind of inquiry and action it desires, their strong degree of engagement may preclude their involvement in genuine CBPAR as the donor may value more traditional forms of inquiry. This donor likely will threaten or subvert the precarious values of CBPAR and may be unwilling to fund less traditional aspects of CBPAR.

<u>Type II Donor </u>(Engaged with a Weak Perspective)

Donor orientation. The donor is well motivated to engage in the project and recognizes its relevance and the value of learning from a given CBPAR project. The donor, however, does not have a firm perspective on the project and its purpose, and may often times appear aimless with regard to the specific action and knowledge generation goals of the project. The donor often has little experience with the CBPAR process and requires of the participant considerable guidance.

For this donor, engagement in the research process of a given CBPAR project may be a product of their own interests in their local community, underscoring the outcomes they seek for this community given the investment of the resources it makes. However, the donor understands the limits of their knowledge of the local community and recognizes the CBPAR project as an opportunity to learn about how participants come to see sound community development.

Participant orientation. Participants in the CBPAR project build the capacity of the donor to serve as an essential stakeholder and through their involvement will advance their competence as a participant. CBPAR personnel support the donor and offer education, technical assistance, and clarification to guide the development of the donor as a participant.

Consonance. This donor may be an effective partner given their significant interest in the work at hand. The donor's weakness of perspective potentially renders them open to CBPAR and to community members' perspectives. This donor may thus protect the values of CBPAR because they depend upon community and other partners to influence the direction of the work. Given the strength of its perspective, this donor may additionally be willing to fund key aspects of CBPAR if community participants are able to effectively represent the significance of these steps to the achievement of shared overarching goals.

Dissonance. Given the weakness of this type of donor's perspective, it is unlikely that dissonance is a significant issue when working with engaged donors with a weak perspective. However, it is possible that this type of donor has some preconceptions regarding inquiry and action that may impact some of their interactions with participants. This likely will not threaten the values of CBPAR as community partners can easily guide the work. However, if the donor does have a weak, yet traditional perspective, they may be unwilling to fund aspects of CBPAR such as relationship building.

<u>Type III Donor</u> (Disengaged with a Strong Perspective)

Donor orientation. The donor does not seek engagement in the project and sees its design and execution as the responsibility of the participants. However, the donor knows what it wants in terms of action and knowledge generation and they frame this early on for the personnel. The donor then refrains from involvement, thereby leaving responsibility for the project with those who are administratively responsible for project direction and performance. For this donor, disengagement does not mean that it refrains from stipulating what it wants, and it enforces this through accountability, oversight, and summative evaluation. These activities do not constitute engagement in the actual research project as quasi- or full participants, but reflect administrative tactics for the enforcement of perspective.

Participant orientation. The participants' strategy is to maintain consistent contact with the donor, communicating frequently about each step in the process. The project administrators do not allow the donor to remain totally disengaged, but offer timely information and updates about progress, barriers, and issues.

Consonance. Provided that donors and community participants agree on the goals of the CBPAR project, this donor will support some of the values of CBPAR. While collaboration with this donor will fall short of true CBPAR due to their lack of engagement as full partners with community participants, this will not threaten the process. Community partners will thus have a significant degree of autonomy to complete the proposed work and the donor and community partners will ideally achieve shared goals. This donor may also be willing to fund the non-traditional aspects of CBPAR if they can be convinced that the work at hand will contribute to their overarching goals.

Dissonance. Dissonance is unlikely with this donor, as they are less likely to support a community-based project that does not conform to their goals, and they do not have to impose strong methodological perspectives upon participants. In the event that the donor has a more traditional perspective on research and action, this may somewhat influence their approach to CBPAR, but it is unlikely to be a significant influence. However, as with other types of donors discussed above, it is possible that a more traditional perspective may disincline this donor from funding aspects of CBPAR such as relationship building, formation of partnerships, and training participants in research methodologies.

<u>Type IV Donor </u>(Disengaged with a Weak Perspective)

Donor perspective. Not only is the donor disengaged from the project, but their perspective on the undertaking is also weak or neutral. This type of donor provides limited parameters within which research and action is to take place and has limited involvement with the final project. The donor expects the project planners to conceive of its aims and design and to implement it accordingly, mindful of the donor's overarching framework guiding action. The donor expects the project leaders to execute the design with little expectation of their involvement in the process. This leaves CBPAR participants with significant room for interpretation and autonomy when it comes to the planning and execution of their projects.

Participant orientation. The project leaders may become very frustrated during the early parts of the process and may take the project and literally run with it, becoming detached from the donor. While the project leaders consistently communicate with the donor, they may turn their attention to moving the project forward, mindful of the donor's framework, and confident that the donor does not seek to control the project's purpose, theory, or implementation.

Consonance. This donor does not act as a full partner in CBPAR, but it offers community participants a significant degree of autonomy, ensuring that social change goals are readily achieved. This donor does not threaten the values of CBPAR, and, if an effective argument can be made, may be willing to fund less traditional aspects of this form of inquiry.

Dissonance. Given its lack of engagement and perspective, dissonance is unlikely to be an operative here. However, the donor may be unwilling to fund aspects of CBPAR for its own idiosyncratic reasons.

Table 2: Donor typology

<table>
<tr><td rowspan="6" style="writing-mode:vertical-rl">Degree of Engagement</td><td></td><td colspan="2">Strength of Perspective</td></tr>
<tr><td></td><td>Strong</td><td>Weak</td></tr>
<tr><td rowspan="2">Engaged</td><td><u>Type I</u>
The Engaged Donor with Strong Perspective</td><td><u>Type II</u>
The Engaged Donor with Weak Perspective</td></tr>
<tr><td rowspan="2">Disengaged</td></tr>
<tr><td><u>Type III</u>
The Disengaged Donor with Strong Perspective</td><td><u>Type IV</u>
The Disengaged Donor with Weak Perspective</td></tr>
</table>

Examples of Donor Roles within CBPAR Projects

Type I: Engaged Donor with Strong Perspective

CBPAR context. ZD has had experience with this kind of donor in the form of a Scandinavian government-based development organization with an international development focus. In this case, the donor had a particular goal in mind, namely, encouraging gender equity within African communities served by the non-governmental organizations (NGOs) it funded. As such, this donor endorsed the values and belief-system of its nation of origin and was only interested in funding interventions and/or initiatives aimed at meeting its stated goals. The donor's perspective thus shaped and limited the kinds of research and action that could be enacted within the targeted communities. This ensured that all participatory work within these communities was aimed, a priori, at encouraging gender equity. ZD collaborated with one NGO who was being funded by this donor and who was faced with the mandate to improve gender equity in the communities they served. This NGO focused on community and economic development and needed to find ways to modify their programming in order to improve gender equity.

In spite of their strong perspective, this donor did not mandate acceptable research methods or the ways in which the social change action they wanted to see was enacted. Participant involvement and ownership could thus be encouraged as long as these were organized around programming that would meet the donor's eventual goals. In order to ensure that their goals were being met, the donor made regular site visits and kept a relatively close eye on the kind of research and programming that was implemented by the NGO.

CBPAR method. Because of the strength of the method and her understanding of the fact that in order for the social change effort to be successful it needed to be informed by the local community, ZD chose to utilize CBPAR for her work. As an external consultant, and in order to accommodate the donor's perspective, ZD framed all CBPAR within the targeted community around the encouragement of gender equity achieved through the empowerment of women. An extensive literature review as well as prior research conducted in this particular nation informed this focus on empowerment. The action goals of the project were thus partly informed by ZD's prior work in similar communities and did not emerge organically from the targeted community. This was in part a measure of expediency as the donor was not willing to fund the initial phases of CBPAR that would have allowed for a greater exploration of these issues within the local context. This forced ZD to make certain assumptions about the ways in which social change would occur in the targeted community.

Once the goal of women's empowerment as a route to gender equity was identified, ZD involved participants in the design and evaluation of the proposed intervention. In order to develop this project, ZD brought women directly into concept development. This involvement included key stakeholder interviews (including women in the community and NGO employees), observation of and participation in community meetings, review of currently used intervention materials, focus group meetings with women during which current practices and programming were discussed as well as potential modifications that women would find helpful, and time spent with NGO employees and extension workers who were responsible for current program implementation.

Information gleaned from these data sources informed the design of the intervention that was to be implemented within the context of the given community. Finally, once intervention design was complete, significant participant involvement was written into the design. It was envisioned that community members would guide and inform all aspects of intervention development and that this research would eventually contribute to social betterment within the targeted communities. Accordingly, an advisory committee of local women would inform programming design and implementation in order to ensure that their most pressing gender-related concerns were addressed. It was intended that this programming would eventually result in greater gender equity within the targeted communities.

The proposed intervention was intended to build upon programming already put in place by a local non-governmental organization. It sought to leverage functional literacy training that included a focus on gender equity, consciousness raising groups, and key informant perspectives as ways to empower participants and to elevate their status within the targeted communities. The planned programming was intended to increase women's overall sense of empowerment and their access to resources necessary to achieve this end (e.g., literacy, an understanding of their rights, and the skills necessary to advocate for themselves). A process and outcome evaluation would allow for an assessment of the success of the intervention. It was intended that a key component of this evaluation would include an evaluation of women's perspective on the success of the intervention, the degree to which their empowerment was encouraged and realized, the degree to which their empowerment contributed to a improvement to their subjective sense of wellbeing, and their overall satisfaction with the program.

Outcome. Notably, the social change that was to be encouraged through this CBPAR project was intended to meet the goals of the donor, not the participants. In addition, all aspects of the intervention were subject to donor review and donor input. In this case, the donor's perspective held substantial influence with regard to the kind of research and action to be engaged in, and while the research was framed as CBPAR, it did not fully conform to the democratic principles that ideally characterize this work. However, in spite of the strong role played by the donor, ZD worked to include women's voices and perspective as much as possible. Women's perspectives on their community, the ways in which gender inequity impacted them, and the kinds of changes they wished to see entered into programming strategy. Additionally, it was intended that women (as participants) would be involved in the execution and evaluation of the program, even if they were not able to refocus programming away from the encouragement of gender equity.

Consonance and dissonance. Notably, in this case example, while the donor and the researcher were in agreement on the value of gender equity, this was less clearly a goal of community participants. While some concerns expressed by women in the community indicated their desire for greater gender equity, it is not clear that all women and men in the community shared those goals. The donor's perspective was thus certainly privileged above those of participants, and the donor and community members did not necessarily have a shared perspective on what the goals of this work should be. While the donor was open to CBPAR, it subverted the values inherent in this type of work as all work was conducted within a preexisting framework. In this work, there was thus largely dissonance between the donor and community participants.

Type II: Engaged Donor with Weak Perspective

CBPAR context. Relevant here is DM's experience with a local community foundation seeking to increase the availability of high quality supported housing for people with serious mental illness. The foundation was dedicated to advancing the local mental health system after rapid deinstitutionalization brought many people with serious mental illness into the local community. Prompted by inadequacies in the local infrastructure to support these returning citizens the foundation strengthened its programs to facilitate the transition and stabilization of those individuals coping with serious mental illness. Overall, the community in which the local foundation was embedded was experiencing considerable economic decline and social distress. The foundation itself set organizational learning goals to advance its insight into community program development mindful that its own charter had to undergo a change to accommodate a new focus and set of goals. The funding of a community group of consumers of mental health services for the purposes of assessing the housing needs of people identified as seriously mentally ill was an initial step the foundation sought to take. It wanted to better understand the housing needs among the members of this local population who lived in the community after moving out of a local state-operated psychiatric facility. While the donor assumed neutrality concerning research methods, its representatives nonetheless wanted to ensure that the project served the aim of appreciating the current housing quality of people identified as seriously mentally ill and the kind of qualities people sought in their housing to support community integration.

CBPAR method. Respecting the empowerment ideology and aims of the members of the local consumer group, DM worked closely with foundation representatives and participants in creating a research agenda to advance housing for people identified as seriously mentally ill. The foundation was quite deferential to the consumer group's control over methodology. The foundation did appoint a liaison whose responsibility was to capture firsthand the experience of this process and bring back first person accounts to the executive staff of the organization. Thus, the foundation representative was highly engaged in the CBPAR project and was counted among its participants. The foundation representative worked closely with the participants, refrained from dictating key aspects of the project, and established herself as a participant in the process mindful of her role as a co-learner addressing the development of a community resource.

The methodology the group employed involved its members in illuminating the living situations and assessing quality of living environments of people identified as seriously mentally ill through photography and personal narratives. Participants served as both research participants documenting their own housing situations, and as investigators guiding the implementation of the project. The participants controlled questions, design, the collection of images, the capturing of first person accounts of housing quality, subsequent data interpretation, and reporting.

Outcome. In this case of an engaged donor with a weak perspective, the local community foundation was very much concerned with involving as many constituencies as possible in the process of community development. Thus, participation of people with primary experience was of considerable value to this donor. Its representatives, however, did not want to remove themselves from the process since firsthand experience with the concerns of the local communities composing the city was a strategy the foundation used to augment its knowledge base and insight into immediate social issues. For the donor, learning directly from this project was of primary importance, while empowering the participants was yet another benefit. For the donor CBPAR itself was unimportant as a form of research. Both parties, the donor and the participants, wanted rich data about housing, and the donor's perspective on the research method or even the fundamental aspects of the research was of little importance for its representatives.

In evaluating the project, the representatives of the local community foundation found their understanding of the housing situations of people identified as seriously mentally ill to be evocative thereby helping them to learn in a way they could not from more traditional research.

The participants felt that their control over the process of inquiry and the respect they experienced from the donor for exercising their own perspective energized their community building aims. The weak perspective on part of the donor proved to be an asset of this project allowing participants to truly shape a CBPAR initiative with the support of a principal community institution.

Consonance and dissonance. In this example, there was significant consonance between community participants and the donor. This ensured that the values of CBPAR were protected and community members were able to participate as equal parties with those representatives of the foundation who could otherwise come to dominate the research agenda and the process of inquiry. The donor truly acted as a participant in the CBPAR project given their learning aims and their desire to understand in rich ways the housing needs of the intended beneficiaries.

This consonance additionally ensured that this project led to social betterment, which in fact it did. Indeed, the group generated considerable insight into the housing situations of people living with serious mental illness, and their illuminatory methodology, which they chose and further developed, was instrumental in spotlighting actual living situations, the issues that people faced in finding adequate and affordable housing, and the very real problems people identifies as seriously mentally ill faced in the adult foster care system that dominated this particular community. Thus, the project resulted in linking the insights the research produced with a subsequent action agenda to develop decent and affordable housing options.

Type III: Disengaged Donor with Strong Perspective

PAR context. In this case the donor involves a university seeking to leverage the investment of its own research stimulation dollars into the expansion of a project's applications to national funding sources, such as the National Institutes of Health, or major national foundations.

DM and his colleague, Washington, brought into a CBPAR framework a project to investigate the dynamics of homelessness among older African American women and, as a result of this knowledge, developed highly relevant intervention tools useful in helping women leave and stay out of homelessness. The project involved homeless and formerly homeless women in establishing the focus and aims of community research and action through the governance of the research process, and in the design and development of intervention tools and models. First founded as an action research project in 2000, the project evolved by 2003 into one in which the aims and processes of participatory action research were driving the research process.

In 2004, the university host invested considerably in this project stipulating as outcomes a significant return on investment, applications to national funding sources, the successful receipt of funding, and an enhancement of knowledge dissemination through publication. The university based those stipulations on its own aims as a national research institution, and the expectations that its research collectively would address national issues. Thus, while the university was disengaged from the actual project, it stipulated performance measures, and introduced a strong perspective on what constituted 'good research'.

CBPAR method. Through the infusion of funding, the project incorporated rigorous developmental mixed methods into the conceptualization, design, development, and validation of tools and instruments supportive of the overarching recovery framework it sought to create for helping participants leave homelessness and achieve independent living outcomes. The project was able to use the impetus the funding offered to expand the participatory roles of homeless and formerly homeless women. The project incorporated a cycle of instrument development, such as the design of an assessment protocol helping women to communicate their own histories of homelessness, in which participants served as content advisors who ensured clarity of concepts and instrument content appropriate to the lives and experiences of older African American women.

The project incorporated highly structured methods, narrative approaches, quasi-experimental designs, and the use of the arts as vehicles for self-advocacy among women. The multiple methods ensured that the project would fulfill the donor's expectations for rigor, while it enabled participants to offer first person accounts of their experiences with homelessness. The detachment of the donor was pivotal in facilitating CBPAR processes and values, but the stipulation of specific deliverables as a result of funding imbued the project with goals that did not necessarily conflict with those of the participants but that nonetheless introduced into the project a different kind of goal set which, in turn, influenced the research culture of the project. Ultimately, to resolve the tension this funding created, the project not only evolved in terms of mixed methods, it evolved through the introduction of mixed models in which participatory methods and traditional research and development were unified in terms of aims, specific subprojects, and project governance.

Outcome. The 'strong perspective' of this donor actually facilitated the outcomes of the project. Emerging over the course of the funding cycle was the project governance or steering council, a community education exhibit on the causes and consequences of homelessness among older African American women, a suite of highly relevant assessment tools, a model of mutual support groups, and a distinctive approach to housing advocacy designed specifically for older women. Two applications for federal funding emerged from this process satisfying the donor's interest in augmenting its own institutional research portfolio.

Consonance and dissonance. There was consonance between what the donor and the participants wanted to achieve. While on the face it may seem that there would not be significant consonance in this kind of partnership, it was the case that both participants were able to achieve their desired goals and were able to do so with mutual benefit. In this case, consonance was strategically leveraged in order to support values of CBPAR and to ensure a positive outcome for all involved.

Type IV: Disengaged Donor with Weak Perspective

CBPAR context. In this case, ZD initiated a needs assessment with Muslim refugee women resettled to the US from Iraq and Afghanistan. Both staff at the local refugee resettlement agency and local Department of Health and key stakeholders in the local Muslim community were concerned that refugee women's needs were not adequately being met. These women experienced resettlement in a gendered manner, but this was not necessarily reflected in the services they received. These services were still largely aimed at men. In this example, research and action was thus initiated.

In order to inform improved programming to this population and to address the concerns raised by the community, ZD proposed a needs assessment with the women. The needs assessment would lay the foundation for programming that would better serve the needs of refugee women and would facilitate their resettlement experiences and their overall health and wellbeing in resettlement. This programming would then be directly informed by the needs and perspective of the local community and would be locally appropriate.

In order to support this work, ZD sought funding from a foundation associated with a local corporation. This foundation was broadly interested in funding health related research of benefit to its home state located in the United States and allowed for significant room for interpretation of its intentions. Finally, the donor's involvement with the project was limited and included review of the proposal and the receipt of a mid-term, and final report. The investigator thus had significant leeway in order to conduct research and inform action.

CBPAR method. This investigation represented CBPAR in a fairly pure form as it was initiated as a result of a need identified by community partners who were also significantly involved in all aspects of research execution. The partners, who were key stakeholders in the local Muslim community and refugee resettlement agency staff, framed the substantive content of research questions, assisted in selecting the sample, assisted with participant recruitment, and collaborated in measurement design. Community partners also participated in data collection (acting as participant recruiters and translators) and reviewed, validated, and approved all findings. This project incorporated a true collaboration between the investigator and members of the community and allowed for a reasonably democratic distribution of power in all key steps and decisions.

This was accomplished through regular meetings with key stakeholders. Initial discussions with stakeholders allowed for the identification of key areas of need. Following those discussions, brainstorming sessions with community stakeholders informed all data collection methods and instrument design. While ZD had the necessary expertise to ensure that all research methods and related instruments were rigorous and valid, community members were able to guide the process to ensure that the methods were culturally appropriate and relevant to women's experiences. Community members additionally reviewed and edited the data collection instrument with an eye to achieving cultural and linguistic appropriateness. Finally, once data collection was complete, meetings with local stakeholders allowed for a validation of all findings. These were then shared with the local refugee resettlement agency, Department of Health, and local community leaders with the goal of altering programming aimed at Muslim refugee women.

Outcome. The disengaged donor with a weak perspective thus allowed for a form of research-participation-action consistent with classical CBPAR. The donor's culture permitted broad interpretation of its perspective, one providing the possibility for the implementation of a wide range of CBPAR projects, even though the donor historically funded traditional research. The donor's lack of involvement in any real aspects of the research additionally ensured that the community's perspective would be salient and therefore the investigator took the opportunity to make them central to the research enterprise. This ensured that any resultant action would be an expression of the needs and perspectives of community members.

Consonance and dissonance. This project was a success largely due to the fact that the consonance between the donor and participants' goals was weak. The donor's disengagement was a significant strength of the project as this allowed participants to steer all research and action in a direction that was consonant with community goals, while still ensuring that the donor's overarching goals of health promotion were addressed and fulfilled.

A Cautionary Tale: Implications for Resource Development in CBPAR

Our experiences with various types of donors illustrate the importance of taking the donor's perspective into consideration when planning and executing CBPAR. The reality is that eventually most research and action requires more funding than what is likely available locally. However, the process of applying for and/or accepting funding may require significant trade-offs participants or stakeholders must make in terms of the CBPAR process. These trade-offs may start as early as the process of identifying donors who are willing to support the work to be completed. In other cases, research and action may be designed specifically in response to donor priorities and may or may not reflect true community needs.

In the case of an existing collaborative, identifying a donor whose values are in line with those of the CBPAR participants may be no easy task. This may require compromises on the part of the CBPAR participants before an application for funding is even submitted. In addition, the type of donor from whom funding is solicited may have equally important implications for the work to be done. As illustrated by the examples we offer previously, as key stakeholders in the CBPAR process, donors may force significant compromises on CBPAR participants by amplifying the importance of substantive or process oriented values. However, in other cases the donors may facilitate the execution of successful CBPAR. As such, donors may have a positive or a negative impact upon the execution of CBPAR. Some donors may thus completely subvert the CBPAR process, while others encourage its viability or foster its emergence.

Notably, the mere fact that a donor is highly engaged does not result in an undemocratic CBPAR process. Engaged donors may be more than willing to allow CBPAR participants to control the process of inquiry and action and may frame their involvement with the process accordingly, often times seeing their own involvement as a form of learning rather than oversight. It is the donor with a strong perspective that may prove damaging to the integrity of CBPAR. Those donors who are unwilling to be reflexive regarding their perspective, goals, and values and modify them in interaction with project participants and community stakeholders simply weaken the spirit and substance of CBPAR.

Donors with a strong perspective can believe strongly in the 'rightness' of their goals and are committed to changing the world in order to align it better with their perspective. Inserting their own preferences into a local context, and forcing a given CBPAR project to serve as an instrumental case for the change they seek to achieve from a cross section of projects they fund, may be a common practice of such donors. For such donors, this may blind them to the fact that community members likely possess very good ideas about the challenges they face, possess clarity concerning the ways in which they themselves can resolve those challenges, and hold well justified preferences concerning the results they seek.

As those examples we offer illustrate, we have had to make compromises to the CBPAR process or have had to be creative in the ways that we engage with donors in order to maintain the integrity of the CBPAR process. Taken as a whole, these examples tell a cautionary tale about the necessity of remaining mindful of the types of donors participants engage in the CBPAR process. While it is possible to engage donors with a strong perspective, this needs to be done in a thoughtful manner where the donor's involvement is deliberately limited to only certain aspects of the CBPAR project (e.g., when funding is needed for a study within the larger project). Our examples additionally illustrate the ways in which a strong donor perspective may subvert the CBPAR process to the point where stakeholders or participant lose or abandon those values that make this model distinctive.

We thus caution CBPAR participants to include an awareness of potential and real donor impacts upon inquiry and action as part of their reflexive processes. We offer this as a suggestion to influence the future praxis of CBPAR, especially for community-based research and action in the interest of social change. Such reflexivity may allow for CBRAR to be more successfully leveraged in the interest of positive social change.

As such, donors and community members may negotiate participatory alliances that leverage resources to optimally address their shared social change goals. In other instances, community members may be able to obtain funding from disengaged donors with a weak perspective in order to forward their goals with little or no consideration of the goals of the donor. In both cases, a critical awareness of the importance of donors' perspective and degree of engagement may influence the outcome of CBPAR projects.

Conclusion: Implications for Theory and Practice in CBPAR

Reflection

CBPAR participants may treat those organizations that provide funding in support of their research and action as silent partners in the research process. However, the truth is that donors can exact a significant influence on the CBPAR process, and their involvement should be problematized. The decision to seek outside funding is thus not one that should be taken lightly. Rather, decisions regarding the kinds of donors with whom they are willing to engage in order to retain the integrity of the participatory process are central to the viability of CBPAR projects.

Additionally, rather than relinquishing significant power over the CBPAR process to donors, participants should expect donors to honor the democratic principles inherent in participatory research and action. Selecting donors with a strong framework of participation in their corporate or institutional framework, or amplifying distinctive values for those donors that do not possess such a framework, are early actions CBPAR projects will want to consider.

This additionally has implications for the ways in which donors choose to frame their funding opportunities and initiatives. As such, the literature on CBPAR can be expanded to take into consideration the roles of donors as participants in CBPAR in order to alter our understanding of this form of inquiry and action. This has important implications for the future of CBPAR and expands this form of research and action to include not only community members and researchers, but also donors.

Implications for Praxis

An awareness of the impact that donors have on CBPAR may have significant implications for the ways in which community members and their research partners go about applying for funding in order to support their work. Including donors as participants ensures that applicants for funding are significantly more strategic about their decisions to pursue funding, the kinds of funding sources they consider, and the ways in which they utilize funding. As such, including donors as participants impacts both CBPAR strategy as well as long-term sustainability of projects. However, this does raise questions about the best ways in which to educate donors about the CBPAR process and the ways in which they could better collaborate with participants. Such education may potentially take the form of a culture shift and increased discussion of CBPAR in publications aimed at donors. Researchers or other donors may author such publications.

Strategy. An understanding of the ways in which donors impact CBPAR ensures that applicants for funding can be strategic about the ways in which they pursue funding. As such, applicants may consider the degree to which their goals are consonant or dissonant with those of potential funders as well as the degree of engagement potential funders may desire. Applicants may then strategically apply for funding from different sources in order to support varying aspects of their work. For example, a donor that has a traditional perspective and expects to have a high degree of engagement may be able to serve as a good source of funding for measurement development, but not for the funding of a larger CBPAR project. In contrast, funding for the initial stages of CBPAR may more effectively be sought from engaged donors who share participants' perspectives and may thus see the value in this process or from disengaged donors with a weak perspective.

If participants in CBPAR pursue funding from donors with a strong perspective, it may be necessary to be strategic in negotiating donor involvement in the CBPAR process, especially if the donor desires a high degree of engagement. This may be complicated for community members who may be more accustomed to relinquishing power and control to donors who they perceive as possessing more legitimacy. This will require community members to see donors as participants who share their goals and partner with them in order to achieve these.

Ideally, donors may also become more reflexive about their goals and more aware of the ways in which they may harness CBPAR to meet their goals. In this case, donors may be more willing to partner with community participants and may be more inclined to protect and support the values of CBPAR in light of the potential of this method. It is thus necessary not only for researchers and community members to alter the ways in which they perceive donors, but donors also need to educate themselves about the value of CBPAR in order to be more strategic about its utilization. In this case, donors would be more willing to fund the non-traditional upfront costs of CBPAR and would be more willing to share power with other participants.

Sustainability. Notably, the funding needs of an ongoing project are different from those required at the inception. This may necessitate the renegotiation of donor relationships or the seeking of new sources of funding. This will then require that participants revisit questions of donor perspective and degree of involvement. These questions are very similar to those asked at the start of a project, except that the sources of funding for this stage of project implementation may be more limited. It may be necessary for participants to give more weight to donor perspectives as it is likely that those donors who fund this stage of project development do so as a result of their own social change goals.

Specific Implications for Donors in Working Effectively with CBPAR Projects

There are multiple ways in which donors may benefit from and better support CBPAR projects. These correspond to the four types of donors identified above.

The engaged donor with a strong perspective. The engaged donor with a strong perspective likely intends to advance a particular social change goal. In this case, the donor may benefit from partnering with community members who have an indigenous understanding of the social concern at hand and may be able to provide a unique perspective that may be of value to advancing the donor's agenda. If this donor is willing to listen to and collaborate with community members, it may be possible to more effectively work towards the achievement of their goals. In addition, the development of community members' capacity may contribute to the long-term sustainability of the social change.

Thus, this type of donor may benefit from treating community members as equal partners who have just as much right to control project design and direction. This donor may want to fund as well as participate in relationship building and planning phases of a community-based project. This would allow the donor to work with community member as a partner while also strengthening the basis upon which their social change goals are built.

The engaged donor with a weak perspective. This donor may want to ensure that community members fulfill their goals (the donors'), but these may be loosely defined. Due to the weakness of their perspective, these types of donors may not wish to actually participate in the various processes outlined above, but may wish to strategically fund aspects of CBPAR. This donor may want to consider funding capacity-building phases or relationship building phases of CBPAR in order to strengthen the outcomes of the projects they fund. The donor's engagement may come from following the progress of all phases of the CBPAR project, as well as a willingness to be flexible in order to facilitate the success of the project. This donor may be engaged in ensuring the success of a project, rather than encouraging particular outcomes.

The disengaged donor with a strong perspective. Similar to the engaged donor, this donor may wish to fund relationship development and other aspects of CBPAR. This donor may be disinclined to participate in the CBPAR process. Given the strength of the CBPAR method, however, this donor may be inclined to fund its unique aspects due to an understanding of the ways in which these aspects strengthen the eventual outcomes of the research and action. Thus, this donor's social change agenda may be advanced through the use of CBPAR even if they are not deeply involved in the process. This donor may thus strategically leverage CBPAR to achieve its goals.

The disengaged donor with a weak perspective. This donor may not have a particular social agenda to advance and may not wish to participate in any aspect of the research and action. However, an understanding of the validity of CBPAR as a research method may ensure that this donor is willing to fund unique aspects of this research (e.g., relationship and capacity building phases). In addition, this donor may wish to have targeted grants such as capacity building or relationship development grants. This would allow participants to utilize funds to lay the foundation for their successful research and action.

Limitations and Areas for Future Inquiry

Perhaps the most significant limitation of the framework we offer in this monograph is its reflexive and preliminary nature. The typology is a product of our own experience and thus it is based on case examples of only two individuals who possess their own perspective, values, and biases. Augmenting this typology so it incorporates the perspectives of other CBPAR participants is a critical step in the illumination of how donors can influence or otherwise contract participatory inquiry. So, through this paper we seek to encourage others to engage in a similar process and to deepen insight into how donors do and can influence CBPAR projects.

Our contribution represents one way of knowing about donors. Thus, as with any knowledge building effort, considerable dialogue, case study, conceptual clarification, and theory development can broaden the knowledge about participant-donor interactions and their consequences for the purpose, integrity, and accuracy of CBPAR in local communities. One of the most significant areas of future inquiry emerging from the development of this typology is empirical validation of our provisional understanding of donor types and of how their perspective and engagement can influence CBPAR. This represents a logical extension of our preliminary process, ensuring that a new praxis may emerge from additional work in this important area of CBPAR practice.

References

Argyris, C., Putnam, R., & McLain, D. (1985). *Action science.* San Francisco: Jossey-Bass.

Boeck, D., Moxley, D., Wachter, H., & Rosenthal, C. (2010). Participatory design in positive aging: Products of the First Cycle of an Environmental Design Action Research Project. *Proceedings of the 2011 Conference of the Environmental Design Research Association.* Chicago, Il.

Bohm, D. (1994). *Thought as a system.* London: Rutledge.

Bronfenbrenner, U. (1981). *The ecology of human development.* Cambridge, MA: Harvard University Press.

Buccola, S., Ervin, D., & Yang, H. (2009). Research choice and finance in university bioscience. *Southern Economic Journal, 75*(4), 1238-1255.

Feen-Calligan, H., Washington, O., & Moxley, D. (2009). Homelessness among older African American women: Interpreting a serious social issue through the arts in community-based participatory action research. *New Solutions, 19*(4), 423-448.

Flicker, S., Savan, B., McGrath, M., Kolenda, B., & Mildenberger, M. (2008). "If you could change one thing…": What community-based researchers wish they could have done differently. *Community Development Journal, 43*(2), 239-253.

Foster-Fishman, P., Fitzgerald, K., Brandell, C., Nowell, B., Chavis, D., & Van Egeren, L. (2006). Mobilizing residents for action: The role of small wins and strategic supports. *American Journal of Community Psychology, 38,* 143-152. DOI 10.1007/s10464-006-9081-0

Foster-Fishman, P., Nowell, B., Deacon, Z., Nievar, M. A., & McCann, P. (2005). Using methods that matter: The impact of reflection, dialogue, and voice. *American Journal of Community Psychology, 36*(3/4), 275-291. DOI: 10.1007/s10464-005-8626-y

Garvin, T. (1995). "We are strong women": Building a community-university research partnership. *Geoforum, 26*(3), 273-286.

Gaventa, J. (1993). The powerful, the powerless, and the experts: Knowledge struggles in an information age. In P. Park, M. Brydon-Miller, B. Hill, & T. Jackson (Eds.). *Voices of change: Participatory research in the United States and Canada.* (pp. 21-40). Toronto: OISE.

Green, G. P., & Haines, A. (2012). *Asset building and community development.* Thousand Oaks, CA: Sage.

Harper, G. W., Bangi, A. K., Contreras, R., Pedraza, A., Tolliver, M., & Vess, L. (2004). Diverse phases of collaboration: Working together to improve community-based HIV interventions for adolescents. *American Journal of Community Psychology, 33*(3/4), 193-205.

Israel, B. A., Schulz, A. J., Parker, E. A., & Becker, A. B. (1998). Review of community-based research: Assessing partnership approaches to improve public health. *Annual Review of Public Health, 19*, 173-202.

Lewin, K. (1946). Action research and minority problems. *Journal of Social Issues, 2*, 34-56.

Lewin, K. (1948). *Resolving social conflicts.* New York City: Harper & Row.

Miller, R. L. & Shinn, M. (2005). Learning from communities: Overcoming difficulties in dissemination of prevention and promotion efforts. *American Journal of Community Psychology, 35*(3/4), 169-183. DOI: 10.1007/s10464-005-3395-1

Plumb, M., Price, W., & Kavanaugh-Lynch, M. H. E. (2004). Funding community-based participatory research: Lessons learned. *Journal of Interprofessional Care, 18*(4), 428-439. DOI: 10.1080/13561820400011792

Quigley, D. (2006). Perspective: A review of improved ethical practices in environmental and public health research: Case examples from Native communities. *Health Education Behavior, 33*, 130-147.

Sarewitz, D. (1996). *Frontiers of illusion: Science, technology, and the politics of progress.* Philadelphia, PA: Temple University Press.

Savan, B. (2004). Community-university partnerships: Linking research and action for sustainable community development. *Community Development Journal, 39*(4), 372-384.

Savan, B., Flicker, S., Kolenda, B., & Mildenberger, M. (2009). How to facilitate (or discourage) community-based research: Recommendations based upon a Canadian survey. *Local Environment, 14*(8), 783-796. DOI: 10.1089/13549830903102177

Senge, P., Scharmer, C. O., Jaworski, J., & Flowers, B. (2008). *Presence: Human purpose and the field of the future.* New York City: Crown Business.

Smith, L. T. (2005). *Decolonizing methodologies: Research and indigenous peoples.* London: Zed.

Washington, O., & Moxley, D. (2008). Telling my story: From narrative to exhibit in illuminating the lived experience of homelessness among older African American women. *Journal of Health Psychology, 13*, 154-165.